SIMPLY LEARN TAROT

BY
ANDREW McGREGOR

THE HERMIT'S LAMP PRESS

Thanks

Hanlon, my partner and support in all I do. My kids for inspiring me with the mysteries of life. The Hermit's Lamp for supporting my family and my ability to create this book. Melinda for all your guidance and help. James Wells for your enthusiastic support, shenanigans, and help editing. Renato for all the help in editing.

Copyright

Foreword

If you want to know how to read the cards this book will help you learn to do readings in a very quick and straightforward way. It is the entirety of what I used to teach in my beginner classes. I hope you enjoy it, have fun with it, and learn what you need from it.

The first thing I want you to know is that everyone uses a book, or notes to read in the beginning. Nobody I know has ever memorized all 78 cards' meanings and then started reading. Everyone I know had to work through some uncertainty in their ability in the beginning. The benefit of this book and the share here is that you can use the book to get you reading right away. This will help you practice and practice is what will help you learn the meanings. Perhaps even more importantly practice will help you learn how to do readings.

What I have come to think is the most important thing to learn, and what I love teaching about, is how to read. How do people learn to see the future? How do people learn the power of being compassionate in their readings? How do we handle other people's turmoil? How do we create custom spreads? Access our guides through tarot? I am very excited to teach people the skills I use in my readings with clients. To do that they need to have some kind of starting point if they have not already been working with the cards. This book is that starting point.

There are lots of great books out there on tarot. It seems every week or two something new is being rolled out and most of them are books for beginners. It is pretty overwhelming when folks are getting started and I often get the question "which one should I start with?" This book also solves that question. Start here. Read and work with this book. If you need more information after 6 months with this book you'll be really clear about what you need to add to your practice.

I love tarot. I feel blessed to get to do what I do for a living. Tarot has been a great companion for the last 3 decades. I hope it is a good friend to you. I hope this book helps you get closer to both the cards and yourself.

Thanks

Andrew McGregor

Table of Contents

Simply Learn Tarot by Andrew McGregor

Introduction

The most important thing you need to know in order to learn to read tarot: IT IS SIMPLE! I mean it. If it feels complicated to you now – it won't after you read and work with this little book. I think that if you are drawn to tarot you will also find it easy – if you remember that it should be simple.

Learning the tarot starts with picking a deck, any deck, and then just playing around with the cards and looking at them a lot. Any deck that has 78 cards will do. If you find yourself drawn to a deck with dragons, cats, crystals, esoteric symbols, or pop culture icons – that is the deck you should use. Simple. All decks have their focus and strengths and none are perfect.

Spend time with your deck. Look at the cards. Leave them around where you will see them and be reminded to use them. Like any relationship, neglect will not get you very far.

As you are working with the cards I want you to use your mind and intuition first. Don't worry I will help you learn how to access the cards directly. There is a very simple exercise in the section on doing the reading that will help you tune into the cards. Once you have used your own faculties first then go to these notes for whichever card you are looking at for more specific information. It is really important not to cheat yourself by jumping right to the meanings I have given. You will be a much stronger reader if you are also using your own intuition.

This book is not perfect. It has a limited scope – practical tarot reading. It is rooted in tradition, but does not get into Qabalah, Alchemy, Astrology, or other traditions in any overt way.

Opinions may vary about my choice of meanings from the broader spectrum of possibilities. I accept the imperfection of it and I hope you do too. Better to start and to learn than to over-think it and not start at all. Keep it simple.

Just because tarot is simple does not mean it is not a vast topic. I have been using the tarot for 25 years now and I am still learning new things about working with the cards. Keep it simple by committing to a few simple rules:

- Keep it real. It takes time to acquire knowledge – no one knows it all.
- Be well rounded. It is better to know one thing about each of the cards than it is to know a whole lot about only a few cards.
- Be regular. Better to look at your cards for 5 minutes a day than in a big crunch all at once. This is not a mid-term exam – you are trying to build a lasting base of knowledge.
- Live your life. Tarot is cool, but it is important to have a rounded life.
- Open to the mystery of it. Magic can happen if you are open to it.
- Context is important. Reading for yourself and your friends will get you further faster.

You might want to read that list a second time.

I have laid this book out so you can put your finger on the information you need when you need it. No long list of symbols. No paragraphs or pontificating. No history, just practical direct meanings. I have included a bibliography at the end if you want more info, but do yourself a favour and seriously consider working only from these notes for 6 months.

How to use this book

This book is built very carefully to cover everything that you need in order to do practical readings for yourself or others. Each card is broken down into six sections. Read the descriptions of them that follow and when you are reading jump to the part that best fits with what you are looking for in your reading. If you are reading about money look only at the line that talks about money. I know that this kind of approach might not come naturally to many people, but it will help you learn faster and give clearer readings so please do your best to follow this advice.

If you hit a word that you don't know the meaning of, check the glossary at the end it is probably hanging out there with a definition.

Title

In the well known Golden Dawn system the cards are given titles. In the Thoth deck, a descendant of this system, these titles are boiled down to one word. So the two of wands, "Lord of Dominion," is called "Dominion" in the Thoth deck. Many other decks will give the creator's title or name for the card. If you are using a deck that has another title you like better add it in the notes or beside the title I have given. It is your personal journey with the cards here. These titles often help people access their memory. They can also be great things to meditate on, especially with the trumps, to get deeper connections.

Association

One of the great strengths of the tarot is its ability to draw connections between a world-wide range of symbols. If you look at the Fool card you will see it is associated with the element Air. It is not that the Fool is made of air or can be substituted for the element itself, but that they share qualities with each other. The wind is uncontrollable. It can be harnessed with windmills to create energy, but it has no real direction of it's own. Storms are unpredictable in part because the wind that moves them is unpredictable. The Fool shares these traits of unpredictability.

These associations are helpful sometimes as triggers for intuitive connections. The Death card, associated with Scorpio, might be talking about a Scorpio in the reading. Don't get caught up in looking for these connections – they will jump out at you when they are relevant.

People with a background in astrology will be able to use the association to bring in the knowledge they already posses about planets, signs and aspects to jumpstart their learning.

Keyword

Keywords are often used as memory aids to help people access what they know about the cards. I have never been fond of them personally as I find sometimes people never go further than one word meanings for the cards when they talk about them. If you don't get caught in that trap they can be helpful. My suggestion is to replace them with your own words as they come to you. Any set of keywords should only be taken as suggestions and not as canon.

General Meanings

As I have said the card's meaning should always be anchored in the meaning of the position where you find it. There **are** times where you won't have a clear meaning (like obstacles, solutions, or allies). If you are doing a daily card draw, for instance, there is no specific context – in this case these general meanings might be helpful. If you are reading a card in a context look first at the *"specific meanings by topic"* section described next.

Specific meanings by topic

These meanings cover the more common questions asked. If you are asking about love use the meaning for love. Simple. You will add a second layer of meaning to it which will come from the position it falls in the spread. We'll get to that soon.

I am quite serious when I say that if you read using the specific topics based on the topic you are reading about you will be on the right track. Watch for the urge to start pulling in lots of other information from other parts of the card descriptions. Less is more most of the time in reading the cards. A simple and direct answer will be heard more clearly, be easier to remember, and is more likely to be acted on.

Yes or no answer

The cards are not good at giving 'yes' or 'no' answers. I don't advocate it in general, but i know that many people will do it regardless. Heck, I do it and I don't even recommend it. So, in the name of not denying something people are likely to do anyway I have included some yes/no suggestions. If you are asking a yes/no question draw one card and refer to this line. You will find some of them are 'maybe's and some are just plain ambiguous. If you don't get a good answer ask another day and leave it alone. I think that there is a kind of obsessiveness that is not healthy that can come from following a yes/no question with a litany of, "what if I do this instead?"

Notes section

Keep track of your ideas about the cards. I'd suggest you include insights about the cards, things that came up in readings, how cards felt in specific contexts. Be mindful to not break confidentiality here. No one will be happy if they find your note "Uncle Bill is the Devil card" by accident. The more you build your own language and connections the more you will master your relationship to the cards.

The Structure in the Cards

The cards are usually divided into 3 categories, the Major Arcana, Minor Arcana, and the Court cards. I would not suggest you get to caught up in drawing distinctions between these three kinds of cards, but I do want you to have some ideas about them.

The Major Arcana are big events. Usually there are 22 of these in a tarot deck and they have names like The High Priestess, The Magician, or The Tower. They tend to be deep moments or events that leave marks or transform us. The Minor Arcana are the how and what. They are numbered from Ace to 10 and are found in four suits often named Wands, Cups, Swords, and Disks. They are the day to day events and interactions. The Court Cards are the who. Most commonly named Kings, Queens, Princes, and Princesses. They are the people or personality traits involved in what you are reading about. They need to be read as people or personality traits that are at play in the situation. The position you find them in will tell you if they are a help or hinderance.

As I said don't get too caught up in these distinctions. They are general guidelines. If it pops into your mind while reading great, but don't spend to much time thinking about them.

Also some decks have varying names for the cards. If your deck does not match exactly with the names I have given, check the table at the back for suggestions on how they line up.

How to practice reading

Do a Daily Draw

I usually do a daily draw with the cards. I pull two cards. One for how my day will go, the second for advice for how to approach my day. I make mental notes about what I think the cards mean for me that day. I then review them either in the evening or before the next day's draw. If you are a journaler then I would suggest writing them down in your journal.

This will help you move through a spectrum of cards quickly. Though you might be surprised at how many repeats you get. It will also get you thinking about tarot in context which will help you understand it more deeply.

Read for Everyone You Can

Everyone starts working from a book or notes. The sooner you get the ball rolling with actual people the better. Do not misrepresent yourself as being a pro, but do not expect it to suck either. Start with people who feel safe, but try to grow beyond that too. I know that I gave myself the best readings ever when I started – well so I thought. As I read for others more I got a better sense of what I was doing better or worse and how to become better as a reader.

Approaching the Cards

When you are doing a reading or looking at your card of the day I want you to ask yourself the following questions before you look at the notes. Seriously. You will cheat yourself and slow your progress by not thinking and feeling before you read from the notes. Remember to be a good reader you have to be willing to be wrong.

1. How do you feel about the card when you look at it in this context? Just a feeling. Happy, sad, worried, satiated, etc. A one word answer is best here. Keep this in mind as you interpret the card as it will guide you about what is going on around this card.

2. What does this card make you think? Are there people in the card? Are they trustworthy, in love, or not talking? Feel free to think and use many words about this one. Tell a little story if you want to.

Do you see how 1 & 2 get your heart and mind working together, but within their own realms of influence? Over time you can also ask yourself what you remember about the card, but don't start with this ever. It will make you sound like a book and can be alienating to folks you are reading for.

The Spread

Do you remember we are keeping this simple? I want you to only use 1 spread for the first 6 months. If you go online you can probably find a different spread for every day of your life. Don't do it. Spreads are helpful once you have some experience, but are a trap for many folks. If you use this spread well and really understand how to interpret the cards in the context of their positions you will be able to pick up any spread and work it without challenges.

Read through the whole description of the spread. Don't get stuck in thinking it is getting complicated—it really is simple. I have included some sample readings below to help make it all clear.

Five Positions of the cards
1. Where the person is coming into the reading. This can include the past, the now, their concerns, and what is going on in general for them.

2. **Obstacles.** What is the block, challenge, opposition, idea, thought, belief, or wall that is between them and what they'd like their life to be like. Any card in this position is an obstacle, even if it is a positive card.

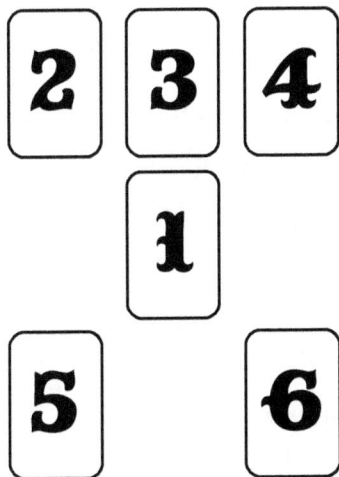

Let me give you an example. The 10 of cups is called satiety and is about complete fulfillment. Cards do not come much nicer than this one. If it shows up as an obstacle we are duty bound to read it in some way as negative, but still keep the actual meaning of the cards in mind. In the obstacles position it can be about expecting too much, being impractical about details, emotions driving things, or the fact that from a peak experience there is often no where to go but down. All of these meanings are in line with what this card could mean in the obstacles section.

A negative card, say the 10 of Swords "Ruin" can be read without needing to modify its already bad meaning. In the case of the 10 of Swords we get as a general meaning "Being stabbed in the back" which is already an obstacle. No need to add extra layers of bad to a bad card in the obstacles position they are usually pretty clearly obstacles already.

Sidebar – Reversals

You might notice that I do not read with reversals. First, learning two sets of meanings is not simple and if you recall this is about keeping it simple. Second, often I feel that reversals miss the nuances of a more context driven interpretation of the cards. ***Contention alert** – many folks will disagree with this if they are on the reversals side – they are right too, but well, this is my book.* How do you read a reversal in a position about obstacles? Does the 10 of swords, called ruin, reversed become success? If it is the obstacles section does this reversal reverse again? I just turn reversals upright to show the client and go on with my business. Keep it simple—if you are going to use this book—and do the same.

3. Solutions. I often call this the "what to do to get the best outcome possible" section. Each card in this section should be read as task, mindset change, action, conversation, or behaviour modification that the person getting the reading should work on to get them where they want to go. Though it may involve other people the actual action needs to be implemented by the person getting the reading.

4. The Future. This is the section about the outcome. What is the person going to get, or what will their life look like if they follow the advice of the reading. Be cautious about being fatalistic about this. The future for the most part is a sea of probabilities, not a narrow road we are forced to walk. Also be aware that the further something is in the future the more changeable it likely is. The closer to the now it is the less changeable.

5. Advice. General things for the person to keep in mind. This is often the most intuitive part of the spread for me. Let it fly here if it wants to fly.

6. What Can't Be Changed. We cannot change everything. Our job might just suck and we are not in a position to move to a new one. Our partner may be a jerk, but think they are the best person ever, making it tough to work on things with them. We might have a flaw that we need to monitor, but can't overcome at this time, or maybe ever. Alcoholics need to stay on top of their drinking, people with tempers have to control them.

This position speaks of what we must accept, work with, work around, or monitor and keep in check.

When you start I would only put one card in each position. As you feel more confident you might want to add a second or eventually a third to each position. Keep it simple and only do this if you find you are not getting clear enough answers. It is not necessary to add cards. I like a lot in my spreads, but it really has its pros and cons.

Okay? What are you waiting for, let's put it all together.

I have created a few sample readings to help demonstrate how it all comes together. I find reading about readings often seems too vague or lacklustre. It will not feel that way when you have a person with a whole set of contexts, emotions, hopes and fears. They will find it speaking to them even if you are not sure what it all means.

Sample 1

The Question is "What do I need to know about this new business product I am releasing?" We know that this is a question about business, so I will look at the line marked money in each of the cards that come up in this reading.

Position 1 turns over the **Death card.**This is the card for where the person is coming into the reading. I look at the meaning for money and it says "change will bring renewed flow." So we can say that this project has a favourable start because more flow in business means more ease and therefore success.

Position 2 gives us the **Princess of Cups.** This position speaks of the obstacles to being successful or getting the outcome we would like. This card speaks of being " a great helper," "only valuing what you do for others," and "giving and nurturing." Notice how they are all about helping others and not about the person doing the giving. The obstacle to this product is in the giving. If the person thinks about themselves too much it will not go well.

Position 3 gives us the **Strength card.** This position is about solutions and actions to take. The line about money says to us "profit comes from hard work." This product will bring work – we talked about flow – but they must work hard to benefit from it.

Position 4 gives us the **5 of Disks.** This card is the is the future or outcome. We look at the meaning for money and it says "debt, fear, anxiety, but a roof over your head." This project is going to bring emotional turmoil. It will provide money, a roof over your head, but perhaps not the ease that it is hoped for.

Position 5 gives us **The Tower.** This position is for advice. When we look to the line about money we see "Bad news." As advice we can ask them how they are prepared for bad news. Since this is the intuitive section in the reading we might branch out and ask "what else is going for you around money?" Remember this is the section to be more open and liberal with your interpretations.

Position 6 gives us the **King of Wands.** This is the section for things that cannot be changed. When we look to the meaning we find "Pure energy," "Putting all one's eggs in one basket," "Being unable to recover if you miss the mark," and "Being in a hurry." The card speaks of overcommitment, being rushed, and only getting one shot at it. The person has to be triply careful in this project. Any mistake can bring failure. Any mistake cannot be corrected. Now at this point the person getting the reading might want to reconsider their approach. Rethink their project. Get clearer about what could go wrong.

This is how we can read for any question. I want to show how it might be different if the same cards came up, but for the question "What can I do to find a great partner?"

Sample 2

If the person is asking "What can I do to find a great romantic partner?" we need to read the meanings about love.

Position 1 turns over the **Death card.** This is the card for where the person is coming into the reading. I look at the meaning for love and it says "ends in heartbreak – self-destructive choices." So we can say that this person needs to take care of themselves and look at the choices that they have made that were not good for them. They have made bad choices in the past.

Position 2 gives us the **Princess of Cups.** This position speaks of the obstacles to being successful or getting the outcome we would like. This card speaks of being " a great helper," "only valuing what you do for others," and "giving and nurturing." Notice how they are all about helping others and not about the person doing the giving. We can build on what we saw in the last card and talk about how they are giving too much.

Position 3 gives us the Strength card. This position is about solutions and actions to take. The line about love says to us "chemical attraction." Desire and passion are the keys to being with the right person.

Position 4 give us the **5 of Disks.** This card is the future or outcome. We look at the meaning for love and it says "money issues, afraid of leaving but might be best." Watch for issues with money making something go bad. Also don't stick around if things are not going well.

Position 5 gives us **The Tower.** This position is for advice. When we look to the line about love we see "sudden end – little chance of renewal." They need to let go of things. Perhaps they continue to try too hard even after it is obvious to the world that things are not going to work out.

Position 6 gives us the **King of Wands.** This is the section for things that cannot be changed. When we look to the meaning we find "Pure energy," "Putting all one's eggs in one basket," "Being unable to recover if you miss the mark," and "Being in a hurry." The card speaks of overcommitment, being rushed and only getting one shot at it. The person has to go slowly, because if they don't it will only make them unhappy.

Looking at your *Card of the Day*

In looking at the card for our day we look to the whole meaning of the card. One line might stand out – go with your intuition. All of them might apply at different points of the day. So the meaning for love, money, and spirit might all come into play. It might seem really vague at first, but after a few weeks your intuition will dial into what is going on, and it will be very powerful.

So if I get the **6 of Disks** I'll look at the whole meaning and keep it in mind.

> 6 of Disks
> Winning
> Title – Success
> Getting what you set out for
> A good end or goal
> a good partner
> solid health
> success
> spirit will guide you to what you need
> positive

So I can assume it's going to be a good day since it is called "success" and all the meanings are positive. I might want to pay attention to my goals since it says "Getting what you set out for." If I had something big going on that day I would feel heartened about it.

Each daily card can be looked at in this way.

Simply Learn Tarot by Andrew McGregor

Major Arcana

Here is a quick reminder of the information given for each card in this section.

Association – standard relationships, often astrological

Keyword – A one word summary of the card

General Meanings – An overview of the nature of the card

Love – Read this line if reading about romance or relationships

Health – Physical, mental, or emotional health

Money – Anything to do with business, money, career, or work

Spirit – For spiritual questions

Yes or No? – If all you need is a thumbs up or down answer

O | **The Fool**

Association	Associated with Air
Keyword	Meandering
General Meanings	Freedom A new beginning Going where the wind blows Lack of discipline Travel
Love	Unstable and uncertain
Health	Senility, lack of focus, ADD
Money	Lack of direction
Spirit	Be in the now
Yes or No?	Anything could happen

Notes

Simply Learn Tarot by Andrew McGregor

I | The Magician

Association	Associated with Mercury
Keyword	Mastery
General Meanings	Focus and balance Knowing what one wants Using truth and illusion to one's ends The ability to make things happen Knowledge
Love	Make it happen – communication is key
Health	You can heal it
Money	Be the boss
Spirit	Be true to yourself
Yes or No?	Positive

Notes

Simply Learn Tarot by Andrew McGregor

II | **The Priestess**

Association	Associated with the Moon
Keyword	Intuitive
General Meanings	Connection with the highest truth Intuition The big picture The Goddess
Love	Maternal love
Health	Positive – female cycles
Money	Intuitive approach will help
Spirit	Be quiet and listen
Yes or No?	Positive

Notes

Simply Learn Tarot by Andrew McGregor

III | **The Empress**

Association	Associated with Venus
Keyword	Loving
General Meanings	Nurturing Giving of oneself Service to others Motherhood and pregnancy
Love	Giving and supporting
Health	Take care of self first
Money	Comes from creativity
Spirit	Service, giving nurturing
Yes or No?	Positive

Notes

Simply Learn Tarot by Andrew McGregor

IV | The Emperor

Association	Associated with Aries
Keyword	Power
General Meanings	Balance of freedom and responsibility Order and structure Consideration for others Pride, Authority, and War
Love	Potential power issue
Health	Positive sign
Money	Promotion, being the boss
Spirit	Balance rules and play
Yes or No?	Positive

Notes

Simply Learn Tarot by Andrew McGregor

V The Hierophant

Association	Associated with Taurus
Keyword	Teacher
General Meanings	Knowledge and learning A teacher or guide Initiation Hard work Help from others
Love	One person is helping the other
Health	Neck, shoulders, ears, and throat
Money	Hard work will help, look for mentor
Spirit	Look to those who went before
Yes or No?	Positive

Notes

Simply Learn Tarot by Andrew McGregor

VI | **The Lovers**

Association	Associated with Gemini
Keyword	Choices
General Meanings	Artificial relationships Marriage without passion The structure put first Duality instead of unity
Love	Commitment if single – if in a committed relationship problems
Health	The arms, lungs
Money	Choices to make – don't sit on the fence
Spirit	Make spirit a part of your life
Yes or No?	Neutral

Notes

Simply Learn Tarot by Andrew McGregor

VII | **The Chariot**

Association	Associated with Cancer
Keyword	Spirit
General Meanings	Connection with the divine Being on the right path Help from above Balance moves us forward Travel
Love	A good match – maybe destiny
Health	Improving – chest and breasts
Money	Comes from respecting spirit and expansion
Spirit	Being on the right road
Yes or No?	Positive

Notes

Simply Learn Tarot by Andrew McGregor

VIII | Justice (Adjustment)

Association	Associated with Libra
Keyword	Truth
General Meanings	Balance and a return to balance Legal troubles Look before you leap Karmic law
Love	Problems – divorce
Health	Need to find harmony with body – kidneys
Money	Make sure to get legal advice
Spirit	Balance life & Spirit
Yes or No?	Neutral

Notes

Simply Learn Tarot by Andrew McGregor

IX The Hermit

Association	Associated with Virgo
Keyword	Seeker
General Meanings	Retirement from the world or isolation
	Seeking knowledge inside oneself
	Guiding by virtue of doing one's own will
	Associated with the hands
	By silence comes inspiration
Love	Being alone
Health	Stomach
Money	Only follow own advice
Spirit	Retreat – meditate
Yes or No?	Neutral

Notes

Simply Learn Tarot by Andrew McGregor

X | The Wheel of Fortune

Association	Associated with Jupiter
Keyword	Change
General Meanings	Change is stability Carefree fun and amusement Expansiveness Good fortune in whatever it is talking about Random events and synchronicity
Love	Change
Health	Positive if person is working on it, negative if not – often stress
Money	Change from current situation
Spirit	Karma and patterns repeating
Yes or No?	Usually positive or neutral

Notes

Simply Learn Tarot by Andrew McGregor

XI | Strength (Lust)

Association	Associated with Leo
Keyword	Strength
General Meanings	Purity taming the beast The joy of strength exercised A sexual relationship Passion in any area
Love	Chemical attraction
Health	Increasing – exercise is important – circulatory system
Money	Profit comes from hard work
Spirit	Be pure
Yes or No?	Positive

Notes

Simply Learn Tarot by Andrew McGregor

XII | The Hanged Man

Association	Associated with Water
Keyword	Stuck
General Meanings	Being stuck due to attachment The need to sacrifice something one wants The descent of the divine into matter Martyrdom, loss, despair Lack of perspective
Love	Stay or go – decide
Health	Problems – needs to detoxify
Money	Stuck – no change without making big change
Spirit	Give up what your ego wants
Yes or No?	Negative

Notes

Simply Learn Tarot by Andrew McGregor

XIII | Death

Association	Associated with Scorpio
Keyword	Ending
General Meanings	Change at a deep level
	Stagnation
	Self-destructive patterns
	Preparation for something new
	Time, aging, death
	End of a cycle
Love	Ends in heartbreak – self-destructive choices
Health	Genitals and inner reproductive parts
Money	Change will bring renewed flow
Spirit	Look beyond the present
Yes or No?	Negative

Notes

Simply Learn Tarot by Andrew McGregor

XIV | Temperance (Art)

Association	Associated with Sagittarius
Keyword	Higher self
General Meanings	Balance of opposites Scientific method Exploration of the boundaries of self The higher self and intuition The spiritual road
Love	The highest kind of love
Health	Thighs – overall good
Money	Use your intuition
Spirit	Union with spirit
Yes or No?	Positive

Notes

Simply Learn Tarot by Andrew McGregor

XV | The Devil

Association	Associated with Capricorn
Keyword	Slave
General Meanings	Attachment to the material Lies, deceit, and unscrupulous action Taking care of practical matters – manifestation Sex and drugs
Love	Self-centred – only physical
Health	STDs – bones – knees
Money	Don't be a slave – watch for lies
Spirit	Let go of material
Yes or No?	Neutral to negative

Notes

Simply Learn Tarot by Andrew McGregor

XVI | The Tower

Association	Associated with Mars
Keyword	Catastrophe
General Meanings	Unexpected change
	Problems with the ego and arrogance
	Troubles at home
	Correction after reaching too far
	Plans are destroyed
	Chaos
Love	Sudden end – little chance of renewal
Health	Troubles – heart attack, stroke, etc.
Money	Bad news
Spirit	Pride leads to a fall
Yes or No?	Negative

Notes

Simply Learn Tarot by Andrew McGregor

XVII | The Star

Association	Associated with Aquarius
Keyword	Destiny
General Meanings	Destiny and astrology Being on the right path or in the right place Limitless possibilities Visions of the divine feminine
Love	Destiny
Health	Ankles – problems that are genetic – neutral
Money	Positive – but beyond control
Spirit	Look to the big picture – astrology
Yes or No?	Neutral to positive

Notes

XVIII | The Moon

Association	Associated with Pisces
Keyword	Illusions
General Meanings	The long dark night of the soul Other people's doubts getting in the way This is the card of mental illness Illusion A lack of options
Love	Dramatic, problems, affairs
Health	Feet – infection – negative – or long road to health
Money	Long road ahead
Spirit	Be careful of illusions – ghosts
Yes or No?	Negative

Notes

Simply Learn Tarot by Andrew McGregor

XIX | The Sun

Association	Associated with the Sun
Keyword	Freedom
General Meanings	The higher self
	Freedom of expression
	Balance and harmony
	Peace of mind
	The harvest
Love	Great – having children
Health	Good health
Money	Increase
Spirit	Great
Yes or No?	Positive

Notes

Simply Learn Tarot by Andrew McGregor

XX | Judgment (The Aeon)

Association	Associated with Fire & Spirit
Keyword	Accountability
General Meanings	Weighing things out The ending of things Learning from the past Preparation for the future
Love	Problems coming out
Health	Surgery – healing
Money	Make sure you are right
Spirit	Facing God
Yes or No?	Neutral

Notes

Simply Learn Tarot by Andrew McGregor

XXI The World (Universe)

Association	Associated with Saturn & Earth
Keyword	The End
General Meanings	The final end before returning to the beginning Patience The completion of things The end of cycle
Love	Creating perfection or parting ways
Health	The end of illness
Money	Balanced
Spirit	Eden
Yes or No?	Both

Notes

Simply Learn Tarot by Andrew McGregor

Minor Arcana

Here is a quick reminder of the information given for each card in this section.

Association – standard relationships, often astrological

Keyword – A one word summary of the card

Title – A one word definition from the Thoth deck's system

General Meanings – An overview of the nature of the card

Love – Read this line if reading about romance or relationships

Health – Physical, mental, or emotional health

Money – Anything to do with business, money, career, or work

Spirit – For spiritual questions

Yes or No? – If all you need is a thumbs up or down answer

The aces are the seeds of what comes later. They are more like a direction than a map. Since they are simpler I have included fewer meanings.

Ace of Wands

Association   Summer (Cancer, Leo, Virgo)

General   Starting
Meanings   The seed of the new
                    Finding the right focus
                    Setting out on the journey

Notes

Simply Learn Tarot by Andrew McGregor

2 of Wands

Association	Mars in Aries
Keyword	Control
Title	Dominion
General Meanings	An issue of control Being in charge
Love	Power issues
Health	Need to take control
Money	Positive if the person is in charge
Spirit	Lead
Yes or No?	Positive if you are in control, negative if you are not

Notes

Simply Learn Tarot by Andrew McGregor

3 of Wands

Association	Sun in Aries
Keyword	Truth
Title	Virtue
General Meanings	The truth is what is real Being right
Love	Let the truth guide you
Health	Face the facts and do what you can
Money	Have integrity
Spirit	Follow your spirit
Yes or No?	Positive

Notes

_____

_____

_____

_____

_____

_____

_____

_____

_____

_____

_____

Simply Learn Tarot by Andrew McGregor

4 of Wands

Association	Venus in Aries
Keyword	Perfection
Title	Completion
General Meanings	The end of a cycle Rebirth or letting go
Love	Endings
Health	The end of struggle
Money	Changing of levels
Spirit	Let go
Yes or No?	Neutral

Notes

5 of Wands

Association	Saturn in Leo
Keyword	Conflict
Title	Strife
General Meanings	Avoidable conflict A pointless fight Being targeted
Love	Fighting and abuse
Health	Bad health from bad conditions
Money	Jealousy and conflict
Spirit	Avoid fighting
Yes or No?	Negative

Notes

Simply Learn Tarot by Andrew McGregor

6 of Wands

Association	Jupiter in Leo
Keyword	Winning
Title	Victory
General Meanings	Know what the target is Success and winning
Love	Getting what you want
Health	Strength and vigour
Money	Success
Spirit	Growth and power
Yes or No?	Positive

Notes

Simply Learn Tarot by Andrew McGregor

7 of Wands

Association	Mars in Leo
Keyword	Integrity
Title	Valour
General Meanings	Take the high road Fight for what you want
Love	Be careful of others stealing what you have
Health	Avoid things you know are bad
Money	Others trying to stop you
Spirit	Be true to yourself
Yes or No?	Negative

Notes

Simply Learn Tarot by Andrew McGregor

8 of Wands

Association	Mercury in Sagittarius
Keyword	Active
Title	Swiftness
General Meanings	Lots of action Communication is key
Love	Lots of passion
Health	Nervousness – needs to relax
Money	Busy, but maybe not profitable
Spirit	Yogic breathing will help
Yes or No?	Neutral

Notes

Simply Learn Tarot by Andrew McGregor

9 of Wands

Association	Moon in Sagittarius
Keyword	Vitality
Title	Strength
General Meanings	Having the energy to see things through Inner fortitude Will power
Love	Positive, but watch power dynamic
Health	Great
Money	Within your control
Spirit	Strong connection
Yes or No?	Positive

Notes

Simply Learn Tarot by Andrew McGregor

10 of Wands

Association	Saturn in Sagittarius
Keyword	Trapped
Title	Oppression
General Meanings	Don't fence yourself in No way forward
Love	No options
Health	Negative
Money	No room for change
Spirit	Yield to spirit
Yes or No?	Negative

Notes

Ace of Cups

Association	Fall (Libra, Scorpio, Sagittarius)
General Meanings	Spirit Clean the emotions Holy Spirit in action The beginning of love

Notes

Simply Learn Tarot by Andrew McGregor

2 of Cups

Association	Venus in Cancer
Keyword	Play
Title	Love
General Meanings	Love and freedom Playfulness
Love	The best kind
Health	Good
Money	Do what you love
Spirit	Have fun—it can't all be serious
Yes or No?	Positive

Notes

3 of Cups

Association	Mercury in Cancer
Keyword	Plenty
Title	Abundance
General Meanings	Enough for everyone Everything you would want
Love	Great
Health	Positive
Money	Increasing
Spirit	Deep connections
Yes or No?	Positive

Notes

Simply Learn Tarot by Andrew McGregor

4 of Cups

Association	Moon in Cancer
Keyword	Sweet
Title	Luxury
General Meanings	Joy, but with a sour note Imperfect, but enjoyable
Love	Good, but not perfect
Health	Minor complaints
Money	Good outweighs the bad
Spirit	Positive
Yes or No?	Positive

Notes

Simply Learn Tarot by Andrew McGregor

5 of Cups

Association	Mars in Scorpio
Keyword	Spillage
Title	Disappointment
General Meanings	Crying over spilt milk Failure or being unhappy with result
Love	Bad news, infidelity
Health	Addiction, bad health
Money	Loss
Spirit	Holding the negative against God
Yes or No?	Negative

Notes

6 of Cups

Association	Sun in Scorpio
Keyword	Enjoyment
Title	Pleasure
General Meanings	A good outcome Fun and good times
Love	Good, maybe not deep connection
Health	Good health
Money	Easy money
Spirit	Bliss
Yes or No?	Positive

Notes

Simply Learn Tarot by Andrew McGregor

7 of Cups

Association	Venus in Scorpio
Keyword	Illusions
Title	Debauch
General Meanings	Going for things that are not real Too much focus on worldly things
Love	Falling in love with an illusion or wrong thing
Health	Try to take it easier
Money	Don't get caught up in fads
Spirit	Don't talk about your spirit too much
Yes or No?	Neutral to negative

Notes

Simply Learn Tarot by Andrew McGregor

8 of Cups

Association	Saturn in Pisces
Keyword	Stuck
Title	Indolence
General Meanings	Depression Lack of will to move forward
Love	Lack of love
Health	Sickness – usually emotional
Money	Loss and slow times
Spirit	Loss of faith
Yes or No?	Negative

Notes

Simply Learn Tarot by Andrew McGregor

9 of Cups

Association	Jupiter in Scorpio
Keyword	Joy
Title	Happiness
General Meanings	Enjoyment of having one's life in order Calm centred happiness
Love	Great
Health	Good health
Money	Feeling good about money
Spirit	Great intuition and connection
Yes or No?	Positive

Notes

Simply Learn Tarot by Andrew McGregor

10 of Cups

Association	Mars in Pisces
Keyword	Fulfillment
Title	Satiety
General Meanings	Everything you want No room for improvement – a big fall if you don't stay on top of things
Love	Perfection
Health	Great
Money	Everything you would want
Spirit	Growth and faith
Yes or No?	Positive

Notes

Simply Learn Tarot by Andrew McGregor

Ace of Swords

Keyword	Winter (Capricorn, Aquarius, Pisces)
General Meanings	Simplicity Good ideas Black and white thinking

Notes

Simply Learn Tarot by Andrew McGregor

2 of Swords

Association	Moon in Libra
Keyword	Justice
Title	Peace
General Meanings	The end of conflicts Impartial opinion
Love	Peace, but may be a parting of ways
Health	Good with a trip to doctor
Money	Be mindful of the law
Spirit	Non attachment
Yes or No?	Neutral

Notes

Simply Learn Tarot by Andrew McGregor

3 of Swords

Association	Saturn in Libra
Keyword	Broken Heart
Title	Sorrow
General Meanings	Misery, unhappiness and despair Failed dreams
Love	Bad news and heart break – loss
Health	Sickness that cannot be overcome
Money	Betrayal and enemies
Spirit	'Why me God?' God moves in mysterious ways
Yes or No?	Negative

Notes

4 of Swords

Association	Jupiter in Libra
Keyword	Agreements
Title	Truce
General Meanings	Stopping of conflict Avoiding getting into things
Love	The starting of healing or parting ways
Health	End of stress
Money	Moving beyond conflict – may lead to growth
Spirit	What can you bypass?
Yes or No?	Neutral

Notes

5 of Swords

Association	Venus in Aquarius
Keyword	Surrender
Title	Defeat
General Meanings	When you can't win, you should give up Bad ideas
Love	A lost cause
Health	Nervousness and anxiety
Money	Bad ideas – get out now
Spirit	Don't fight against your spirit
Yes or No?	Negative

Notes

Simply Learn Tarot by Andrew McGregor

6 of Swords

Association	Mercury in Aquarius
Keyword	Rational
Title	Science
General Meanings	Right thinking Realistic well thought out plans
Love	Good ideas – might be missing the spark
Health	Do what you know you should
Money	Make a plan or stick to the one you have
Spirit	Don't be flaky or give in to fantasy
Yes or No?	Positive

Notes

Simply Learn Tarot by Andrew McGregor

7 of Swords

Association	Moon in Aquarius
Keyword	Hopeless
Title	Futility
General Meanings	Too many small obstacles No way to win
Love	No big problem, but too many little ones
Health	Lots of small complaints
Money	Squandering cash here and there
Spirit	Don't let the little things get you down
Yes or No?	Negative

Notes

Simply Learn Tarot by Andrew McGregor

8 of Swords

Association	Jupiter in Gemini
Keyword	Gossip
Title	Interference
General Meanings	Gossip, jealousy, and slander Other's words or actions getting in the way
Love	Others get in the way. (An ex or family)
Health	Others have made the problem
Money	Enemies at work
Spirit	Others words block you
Yes or No?	+/- negative

Notes

Simply Learn Tarot by Andrew McGregor

9 of Swords

Association	Mars in Aquarius
Keyword	Depression
Title	Cruelty
General Meanings	Bad dreams, curses, and nightmares Fears and craziness
Love	A bad relationship
Health	Depression and anxiety
Money	Bad luck, bad idea – doing too much
Spirit	Watch dreams for clues as to what is wrong
Yes or No?	Negative

Notes

Simply Learn Tarot by Andrew McGregor

10 of Swords

Association	Sun in Aquarius
Keyword	Betrayal
Title	Ruin
General Meanings	The worst it could get Being stabbed in the back
Love	Horrible, dangerous, maybe violent, issues
Health	Nervous break down, binge drinking etc
Money	Loss of everything
Spirit	Loss of contact with spirit
Yes or No?	Negative – the worst card in the deck

Notes

Simply Learn Tarot by Andrew McGregor

Ace of Disks

Keyword	Spring (Aries, Taurus, Gemini)
General Meanings	Seed The beginning that will lead to fruit Starting to build or regain on a physical level

Notes

Simply Learn Tarot by Andrew McGregor

2 of Disks

Association	Jupiter in Capricorn
Keyword	Shifting
Title	Change
General Meanings	Things go up and down Be ready for change and you will succeed
Love	Change is good if you can go with the flow
Health	Ups and downs, don't forget to pay attention
Money	Season ebbs and flows
Spirit	Change is the constant
Yes or No?	Neutral

Notes

　Simply Learn Tarot by Andrew McGregor

3 of Disks

Association	Mars in Capricorn
Keyword	Industrious
Title	Works
General Meanings	Your success is in your hands You get what you work for
Love	Problems that can be sorted out with work
Health	Take control – consult doctor
Money	Make your own fortune by hard working
Spirit	Discipline and focus required
Yes or No?	Positive

Notes

4 of Disks

Association	Sun in Capricorn
Keyword	Defense
Title	Power
General Meanings	Create or maintain order The need for boundaries
Love	Take care of money to take care of relationship
Health	Exercise and eat right
Money	Be conservative – invest in the future
Spirit	Establish a foundation
Yes or No?	Positive

Notes

Simply Learn Tarot by Andrew McGregor

5 of Disks

Association	Mercury in Taurus
Keyword	Fear
Title	Worry
General Meanings	Anticipating the worst Getting what you need, but not what you want
Love	Money issues, afraid of leaving, but might be best
Health	Don't avoid looking at issues – it can be dealt with
Money	Debt, fear, anxiety, but a roof over your head
Spirit	Conflict between money and spirit
Yes or No?	Negative

Notes

Simply Learn Tarot by Andrew McGregor

6 of Disks

Association	Moon in Taurus
Keyword	Winning
Title	Success
General Meanings	Getting what you set out for A good end or goal
Love	A good partner
Health	Solid health
Money	Success
Spirit	Spirit will guide you to what you need
Yes or No?	Positive

Notes

Simply Learn Tarot by Andrew McGregor

7 of Disks

Association	Saturn in Taurus
Keyword	Losing
Title	Failure
General Meanings	Nothing will work out No success
Love	A relationship that has ended
Health	Sickness building due to lack of attention
Money	Loss and failure, bad management
Spirit	Bad faith
Yes or No?	Negative

Notes

Simply Learn Tarot by Andrew McGregor

8 of Disks

Association	Sun in Virgo
Keyword	Caution
Title	Prudence
General Meanings	Be conservative to succeed Change now before it's too late
Love	Take care of it before it's gone
Health	Deal with problems now while you still can
Money	Be cautious
Spirit	You walk a line between good and bad
Yes or No?	Neutral

Notes

9 of Disks

Association	Venus in Virgo
Keyword	Acquisition
Title	Gain
General Meanings	Growth and expansion Building up
Love	Growth in relationship
Health	Getting stronger
Money	A good job or opportunity
Spirit	Patience and things improve
Yes or No?	Positive

Notes

10 of Disks

Association	Mercury in Virgo
Keyword	Stockpile
Title	Wealth
General Meanings	Money and things Dissipates if not attended too
Love	Great person
Health	Health
Money	Wealth and riches
Spirit	Happiness and bliss
Yes or No?	Positive

Notes

Court Cards

Read the court cards as personality traits or people in the situation. If you are unsure ask the person who this trait reminds them off.

Elements – the combination of the four elements

Phrase – this is like the keyword in the other cards

Astrology – the time of the year that this card goes with

General Meanings – ideas about the nature of the card

King of Wands

Elements	Fire of Fire
Phrase	All or nothing
Astrology	20° Scorpio to 20° Sagittarius
General Meanings	Pure energy Putting all one's eggs in one basket Being unable to recover if you miss the mark Being in a hurry

Notes

Queen of Wands

Elements	Water of Fire
Phrase	My way or else
Astrology	20° Pisces to 20° Aries
General Meanings	Loyalty
	Hot temper
	Manipulative when afraid she won't get what she needs
	Vengeful when crossed, or at the appearance of being crossed
	Strong
	Brave

Notes

Simply Learn Tarot by Andrew McGregor

Prince of Wands

Elements	Air of Fire
Phrase	Easygoing
Astrology	20° Cancer to 20° Leo
General Meanings	A boaster
	Humour can deflect problems
	Don't take yourself seriously
	Courageous
	Good at sales

Notes

Princess of Wands

Elements	Earth of Fire
Phrase	Fiery righteousness
Astrology	Rules the Summer
General Meanings	A just person Fairness being important Righteous in anger and often over-reacting An activist or hero

Notes

Simply Learn Tarot by Andrew McGregor

King of Cups

Elements	Fire of Water
Phrase	Go for your dream
Astrology	20° Aquarius to 20° Pisces
General Meanings	A dreamer Pursuing spiritual goals The need to dream big A wanderer Creative types

Notes

Queen of Cups

Elements	Water of Water
Phrase	Mirror to the world
Astrology	20° Gemini to 20° Cancer
General Meanings	Reflection Blending in socially Showing others what you think they want to see Expecting others to be psychic

Notes

Simply Learn Tarot by Andrew McGregor

Prince of Cups

Elements	Air of Water
Phrase	Fighting not to sink
Astrology	20° Libra to 20° Scorpio
General Meanings	A drunk Unable to let go of the past Fighting to get past stagnation Sneaky or conniving

Notes

Princess of Cups

Elements	Earth of Water
Phrase	The world's helper
Astrology	Rules the Fall
General Meanings	Only valuing what you do for others A great helper Giving and nurturing

Notes

Simply Learn Tarot by Andrew McGregor

King of Swords

Elements	Fire of Air
Phrase	Swift as an arrow
Astrology	20° Taurus to 20° Gemini
General Meanings	A good plan Fast-moving One pointed Pragmatic and driven Attack

Notes

Simply Learn Tarot by Andrew McGregor

Queen of Swords

Elements	Water of Air
Phrase	I am the boss
Astrology	20° Virgo to 20° Libra
General Meanings	A strong woman In control of her emotions Harmony of the head and heart Joan of Arc[1]

Notes

Simply Learn Tarot by Andrew McGregor

Prince of Swords

Elements	Air of Air
Phrase	Around in circles
Astrology	20° Capricorn to 20° Aquarius
General Meanings	Confusion Divided effort Too busy Leaping from task to task without finishing Exuberance of youth

Notes

Simply Learn Tarot by Andrew McGregor

Princess of Swords

Elements	Earth of Air
Phrase	Fighting against the odds
Astrology	Rules the Winter
General Meanings	A defender of others A fighter Activist Vigilant Noble

Notes

Simply Learn Tarot by Andrew McGregor

King of Disks

Elements	Fire of Earth
Phrase	Things happen on God's time
Astrology	20° Leo to 20° Virgo
General Meanings	Day-to-day work Attention to details Things being beyond your control Time of peace Agriculture

Notes

Queen of Disks

Elements	Water of Earth
Phrase	Plant the seed today for tomorrow's reward
Astrology	20° Sagittarius to 20° Capricorn
General Meanings	Waiting Planting the seeds of what's to come Knowing things come in time Success, but not today

Notes

Prince of Disks

Elements	Air of Earth
Phrase	Slow and steady
Astrology	20° Aries to 20° Taurus
General Meanings	Hard working Advancement comes by daily work Focus on your efforts not on other's efforts Simple and earthy wisdom The work of seasons

Notes

Simply Learn Tarot by Andrew McGregor

Princess of Disks

Elements	Earth of Earth
Phrase	Waiting for the new beginning
Astrology	Rules the Spring
General Meanings	Ready for change, but the time has not come Patience The end of things with the seed of what is to come The depths of winter waiting for the spring Careful

Notes

How the names of the suits line up among various decks

Suit	Alternate
Wands	Batons, Clubs, Fire, Pipes
Cups	Chalices, Bowls, Water, Hearts
Swords	Feathers, Air, Spades, Arrows
Disks	Coins, Earth, Stones, Diamonds, Pentacles

How to work with the names of the court cards in other decks

In this book	Thoth Deck	Marseille	Other
King	Knight	King	Elder, Exemplar, Shaman
Queen	Queen	Queen	Guardian, Lodge, Priestess
Prince	Prince	Knight	Seeker, Totem, Son
Princess	Princess	Knave	Child, Apprentice, Daughter

Biography

I have always been interested in the spiritual side of life. In grade school my friends and I, amidst playing ninja in the forests where I lived, also tried to meditate. We would climb into the back of the crawl space at my friend Mike's house and light incense and work on sitting still, breathing and certain gestures we had learned from books about martial arts.

When I was 13 I was in a local mall bookstore with my Grandmother. I saw a tarot set for sale, the Mythic Tarot, and immediately asked her if she would get it for me. Being a loving supporter of my interest in all things, mystical, weird, or macabre, she immediately said yes. It was also around that time that I discovered Aleister Crowley, the Qabala, and ceremonial magick at a local psychic fair. The stage was set.

The next year I was in a serious accident while driving a scooter in the Dominican Republic. I can tell you getting nailed by a dump truck that has decided to pass around a blind corner is no fun. While learning to walk again I also started to ask some big existential questions of the universe. I became voracious in my reading, quickly tearing through all the philosophy, religion, and political books the school library had to offer. I started to try to figure it all out. I was lucky to be supported in my search by my family.

This was all before the internet was around so I started to talk with whoever I could find that was willing to speak with me about it - priests, jesuits, occultists, anyone who would cross my path.

After high school I went to a local art school and studied sculpture. Now that I was living on my own and in Toronto I delved deeper into my spirituality. Looking for groups, and setting myself regular practices working on all the stuff I had started as a child in my friend's crawl space. Yogic breathing, learning to control the body and the mind, moving and feeling energy. I got into martial arts again. I finished art school with a real dislike for the art world in general, but an intense love for religious art.

After university I found my way to doing graphic design and later worked freelancing for many big companies in the financial sector. I met the person who would later become my life partner. My fascination with the spiritual continued to grow. I got initiated into some western mystery schools. I found new friends to do ceremonies with. I traveled to India, spent time with native elders, hosted community retreats, studied counselling, and continued to seek for answers. I came to really dislike my work and jumped like the fool into working as a reader for a website, then a local store, and finally about 6 years ago set out on my own. My partner and I expanded our family with two girls. 4 years ago I opened my own storefront, The Hermit's Lamp, as part of my vision to make available great decks, books, spiritually supplies and really exciting events.

At the time of writing this book I have been reading the cards for about 28 years. For the last 12 years this has been my job and I have been teaching people how to read the cards, qabala, meditation and other tools for the last 5 years.

Would you like more?

I hope that you have enjoyed the book and that it serves you well. I am available for readings and private classes in person in Toronto or from anywhere else by phone or Skype. I teach regular classes in Toronto and webinars for people anywhere in the world.

I write a regular blog about tarot and life, and I also record a podcast (where I interview tarot readers about the big questions around tarot) all on my website: www.thehermitslamp.com/tarot_blog

I am in many of the places you might expect to find me online and invite you to come hang out with me there if you like. You can find me online in the following places:

Facebook.com/thehermitslamp
@thehermitslamp
andrew@thehermitslamp.com

I look forward to hearing from you.
Andrew McGregor

End Notes

1.   **Huson, Paul** (2004) _Mystical Origins Of The Tarot_. Inner Traditions

Glossary

Arcana – Used to describe the tarot. Other words like Atu, Pips, and Trumps might be used.

Association – standard relationships, often astrological

Court cards – Usually 4 cards King, Queen, Prince, and Princess. (see appendix for name variations)

General Meanings – An overview of the nature of the card

Golden Dawn – A system of magic geared towards personal evolution drawing from tarot, astrology, qabala, and many other sources

Health – Physical, mental or emotional health

Keyword – A one word summary of the card

Love – Read this line if reading about romance or relationships

Major Arcana – The 22 cards with names like 'the Tower,' 'the Star,' 'the Emperor.' Also called Trumps.

Minor Arcana – The cards numbered from Ace to 10 in four suits. Sometimes called Pips. (see appendix for variations)

Money – Anything to do with business, money, career, or work

Spirit – For spiritual questions

Thoth deck - A deck created by Aleister Crowley and Frida Harris

Yes or No? – If all you need is a thumbs up or down answer

Bibliography

I have read a lot of books on the cards. It is practically impossible for me to delineate where all of my ideas have come from over the years. I have also read many blogs and have had the great luck to talk with some very knowledgeable folks about tarot. This bibliography represents what I recall as being most important in my development and what can help expand your practice beyond working with this manual. Keep in mind I was really serious when I said think about sticking to only this for 6 months.

Crowley, Aleister. (1944). _The Book of Thoth:_ _A Short Essay on the Tarot of the Egyptians._ Republished (1969). York Beach, ME: Samuel Weiser

DuQuette, Lon Milo (2003). _Understanding Aleister Crowley's Thoth Tarot._ Weiser Books

Huson, Paul (2004) _Mystical Origins Of The Tarot._ Inner Traditions

Wang, Robert. (1983). _The Qabalistic Tarot: A Textbook of Mystical Philosophy._ York Beach, ME: Samuel Weiser.

Nichols, Sallie. (1980). _Jung and Tarot: An Archetypal Journey._ York Beach, ME: Samuel Weiser.

Colbert, Joanna Powell (2011). _The Gaian Tarot,_ Llewellyn Publications

Fortune, Dion (pseud. for Violet Firth). (1935). _The Mystical Qabalah._ Republished (1984). York Beach, ME: Samuel Weiser.

www.ingramcontent.com/pod-product-compliance
Lightning Source LLC
Chambersburg PA
CBHW062004040426
42447CB00010B/1904